50 REASONS TO KEEP ON LIVING

Jonathan Juca

~For Grandma~

Table of Contents

1. A warm cup of coffee in the morning   1

2. Freshly baked bread   2

3. The smell of rain on dry earth   3

4. Waking up naturally without an alarm   4

5. The feeling of clean sheets   5

6. A long, deep hug from someone you love   6

7. Watching the sunrise or sunset   7

8. Laughing until your stomach hurts   8

9. A perfectly ripe piece of fruit   9

10. Finding money in your pocket you forgot about   10

11. Listening to your favorite song on repeat   11

12. A genuine compliment from a stranger   12

13. Walking barefoot on soft grass   13

14. A refreshing breeze on a hot day   14

15. The first sip of cold water when you're really thirsty   15

16. A cat purring on your lap   16

17. A dog excitedly greeting you at the door   17

18. The crackling sound of a fireplace   18

19. Looking at old photos and reminiscing   19

20. A spontaneous adventure   20

21. Receiving an unexpected gift   21

22. Watching raindrops race down a window   22

23. The smell of freshly cut grass   23

24. A great book you can't put down   24

25. Stargazing on a clear night   25

26. Finding the perfect parking spot   26

27. Seeing a rainbow after the rain   27

28. The feeling of accomplishment after finishing a task   28

29. Wrapping yourself in a cozy blanket   29

30. A heartfelt "I love you"   30

31. Watching baby animals play   31

32. The scent of a loved one's perfume or cologne   32

33. The excitement of opening a package   33

34. A handwritten letter or note   34

35. The first bloom of spring flowers   35

36. A perfectly timed joke   36

37. Blowing bubbles and watching them float   37

38. A relaxing bath with candles   38

39. A deep, fulfilling conversation   39

40. The smell of books in a library   40

41. Witnessing an act of kindness   41

42. A favorite childhood movie or TV show   42

43. The feeling of sand between your toes   43

44. A perfectly cooked meal   44

45. The first snowfall of winter   45

46. The satisfaction of popping bubble wrap   46

47. Watching fireflies on a summer night   47

48. Singing in the car with friends   48

49. A cold pillow on a warm night   49

50. Seeing someone light up because of your words or actions   50

Arthur Bio: 51

1

A WARM CUP OF COFFEE IN THE MORNING

The simple pleasure of holding a warm mug, feeling the steam rise, and taking that first sip of rich, bold coffee can set the tone for a peaceful, hopeful day. It's a reminder that even in the midst of chaos, small rituals bring comfort. I absolutely love the taste and the aroma bit on my tongue, and it exhilarates me.

2

FRESHLY BAKED BREAD

The scent of freshly baked bread fills a home with warmth and nostalgia, giving you a sense of security. Each bite, soft and satisfying, is a simple but powerful reminder that good things take time—and that patience is always rewarded. Growing up, I just tried baking a bunch of different breads I've never tasted before, and yeah, they came out different but satisfying each time. Doing that just shows you what you could do if you put your time and patience into something.

3

THE SMELL OF RAIN ON DRY EARTH

That deep, earthy scent after a rainfall is a sign of renewal, of nature's ability to cleanse itself and begin again. It's a reminder that even the driest times in life can be followed by refreshments and new beginnings. I don't really like rainy days, but it was those rainy days, especially during late winter to early spring, that are required so we could receive the new beautiful springtime, flowers, and grass.

4

WAKING UP NATURALLY
WITHOUT AN ALARM

Few things feel as freeing as waking up to the gentle embrace of morning light instead of a blaring alarm. It's a moment of pure peace, proof that rest and renewal come when we give ourselves grace. It's so much better to wake up right before the alarm clock hits, especially before the iPhone alarm sounds. Yeah, I know it feels absolutely refreshing. Especially once I get eight hours of sleep, then I'm good. My whole day has been made just because of that.

5

THE FEELING OF CLEAN SHEETS

Slipping into fresh, crisp sheets at the end of a long day is a small but luxurious pleasure. It's a reminder that even in a fast-moving world, there is always space for comfort and self-care, especially after getting clean sheets, pressing them, feeling every single warmth afterward, and going to bed at a reasonable time. Nothing, it's more than that. It's absolutely phenomenal the kind of sleep I get during those days.

6

A LONG, DEEP HUG FROM SOMEONE YOU LOVE

A hug can say more than words ever could. It's warmth, its safety, it's a physical reminder that you are loved and not alone in this world. Whether that be me giving a hug to somebody else or receiving a hug from a loved one like my mother and father, there's nothing more than having a person be there and just remind you that I think you're gonna be OK. You know, there were points in my life where I thought the whole world was falling apart, but just having a hug from somebody brought me back to reality, I guess, re-framed things, especially during those times.

7

WATCHING THE SUNRISE OR SUNSET

The colors that streak across the sky at dawn and dusk are proof that beauty exists even in the most fleeting moments. Each sunrise is a new beginning, and each sunset is a peaceful close to another day lived. Watching the sunrise. It absolutely gives me so much energy. I'll tell you, it invigorates my day, just being able to feel the light touch up on your skin and gain literally that little vitamin D just flying through you. As for the sunset, it's just good to watch it go down, just knowing that he fulfilled what you came to accomplish that day, and now you are able to rest, knowing that you've done so interesting the sun go down upon the horizon as the colors seem to change from bright yellow and light blue to darker shades like a pink-red orange is breathtaking.

8

LAUGHING UNTIL YOUR STOMACH HURTS

Laughter is one of the purest forms of joy, an uncontrollable reaction to something so unexpectedly funny that it takes over your whole body. It's a moment where nothing else matters, and you are fully present in happiness. There are so many times that I, my older brother, and my younger siblings just laugh at the most minuscule of things until we can barely breathe for a few minutes. Looking back, I forget the entire joke of some of the things, but I remember that feeling of just being so out of breath and just laughing so much that our stomachs hurt, and it reminds me of really great times I had, and I hope to continue to have.

9

A PERFECTLY RIPE PIECE OF FRUIT

Juicy, sweet, and full of flavor, the taste of perfectly ripe fruit is nature's way of reminding us that the best things come in their own time. Yeah, I know. I love eating fruit right when it's ripe. It is fantastic, especially oranges. Oranges are absolutely phenomenal. I remember one time. I went on vacation to Florida and to Mexico and had some of the oranges that were just ripe right from the tree and the fruit just gushing. Delicious!

10

FINDING MONEY IN YOUR POCKET YOU FORGOT ABOUT

It's a little surprise, a small moment of unexpected joy like life reminding you that sometimes, good things come out of nowhere. They came in clutch so many times for me in my personal life. Just one time, I was going out with a bunch of friends to go out to eat dinner, and I found an extra $20 bill in my pocket, and I was like, "Oh awesome, get to have dinner and also a drink too. It's gonna be a great night!"

11

LISTENING TO YOUR FAVORITE SONG ON REPEAT

Music has the power to transport us, to heal, and to energize us. Your favorite song is a safe space, a place where you can let go and just feel. I swear, Apple Music, once you have 10 songs, you can have a playlist with over 1000 songs, but those 10 songs you can always go back to will always bring up your day no matter what. It's such a great way to know that we all have those go-to songs we can rely on to lift us up. I'll give you guys 2 of my all-time repeat songs: Mercy Mercy Me - Marvin Gaye and Square - Yerin Baek.

12

A GENUINE COMPLIMENT FROM A STRANGER

When someone takes the time to notice something good about you and say it aloud, it's proof that kindness still exists in the world. Receiving a compliment feels great, and also giving when also feels great too. Whether it be completing the person's attitude, dress style, or who they are. It's great to receive a compliment from someone, and giving one to another stranger also makes you feel good about yourself. And I hope you receive the same one day as well.

13

WALKING BAREFOOT ON SOFT GRASS

Feeling the earth directly beneath your feet is grounding, a reminder that we are part of something bigger. Especially now that springtime is almost coming, just being able to feel the fresh new grass at the start of the morning and feeling just like a bit of moisture between your toes is great. I can't wait for the warm weather and the sunshine to warm and let the ground grow a vibrant green.

14

A REFRESHING BREEZE ON A HOT DAY

A cool breeze in the middle of the heat is like an unexpected gift—subtle but deeply appreciated, proof that relief always comes eventually. You know that feeling, working outside for hours or going out for a job on a hot day and then, out of nowhere, a fresh cool breeze. That is accompanied by your body trying to cool itself down, AKA Sweet. It hits really differently, especially after working in the sun for a long time. That, paired with a cool fresh and a sip of water, is fantastic.

15

THE FIRST SIP OF COLD WATER WHEN YOU'RE REALLY THIRSTY

Speaking of. That feeling of quenching a deep thirst is one of life's most straightforward yet most satisfying moments, reminding us to be grateful for small necessities. I'm just reeling back to what I said on the last page. Yeah, I know that a fresh bottle of water, especially when you're thirsty or during a hot day, is literally the most refreshing thing you could do that happened throughout the day.

16

A CAT PURRING ON YOUR LAP

The soft vibration of a purring cat is soothing, a signal of trust and comfort. It's a reminder that companionship can be quiet but deeply meaningful. It's funny near where I live. There are many stray cats, and some of them got really comfortable with our neighbors. I remember when I was in school, you could just sit down and call the cat to me, and yeah, they went on top of my lap, and I just sat with them while we waited for the bus to come. Just having a little cat by you waiting for your day to start is really just refreshing. It's really lovely, and it's comforting to have a little companion with you to start the day.

17

A DOG EXCITEDLY GREETING YOU AT THE DOOR

No matter how challenging your day was, a dog's wagging tail and uncontainable excitement tell you one thing—you are loved, you are essential, you are home. Especially after a long day, it's nice to have your dog come running up to you. It's great when you approach the door and are greeted by your dog, and they are able to jump on you excitedly, throwing their entire body on you, especially when they're young. I have so many fun memories of that as well.

18

THE CRACKLING SOUND OF A FIREPLACE

There's something hypnotic about the flickering flames and the gentle crackle of burning wood, a reminder of warmth, safety, and the simple joys of being present. It's great to have bonfires with a bunch of friends and talk, laugh, and joke about many things. That, paired with a beer, water, or other drink, is a great time. Then, the feeling of the fire, especially during a fall evening or early spring day, of feeling the fire in the warmth surrounding you. Exquisite.

19

LOOKING AT OLD PHOTOS AND REMINISCING

Pictures freeze moments in time, allowing us to revisit memories and remind ourselves of all the beautiful experiences we've lived through. The biggest advice I can give a person is to take as many photos as you can for memory. One of my big regrets in life is not taking enough photos some days. So, do you take a lot of photos? That is my most significant piece of advice, and especially when you're looking back at your account at Files or Photos, it'll bring up many fond memories.

20

A SPONTANEOUS ADVENTURE

Unplanned trips and sudden explorations remind us that life is unpredictable, exciting, and full of possibilities. When do you have the time, whether it be a massive vacation or a small trip? Always go on spontaneous adventures, such as heading out to a new hiking trail, going to walk in a new neighborhood, going out to a different country, planning out a whole itinerary, taking a bunch of friends with you, or just going on a solo trip. Just make sure to make your life spontaneous and fun, and always seek wonder. Never forget that feeling of genuine wonder and exploring new things.

21

RECEIVING AN UNEXPECTED GIFT

A surprise gift, no matter how small, is a reminder that someone thought of you, that kindness exists, and that joy can come when you least expect it. Will it be a small piece of gum, a utensil, something that you need in your kitchen cabinet, flowers, a letter, or something thoughtful a person gives you. Receiving a small gift is always so welcome and a reminder of people genuinely caring about you and thinking about you as well.

22

WATCHING RAINDROPS RACE DOWN A WINDOW

Something as simple as watching raindrops slide down glass can be oddly calming, a quiet reminder that even chaos has its patterns. Even when I backseat ride in a car on a rainy day, I always look at some raindrops, and just when I'm sitting in the back, I just watch the raindrops race each other slowly and gently as if they were brothers or sisters.

23

THE SMELL OF FRESHLY CUT GRASS

That distinct scent is a signal of new beginnings—of summer days, open fields, and the simple pleasure of being outdoors. Especially after working in the yard for a couple of hours, you are paid for the job sometimes, and sometimes you are not, but I feel like just the smell of the fresh-cut grass alone is worth it, especially after a hard day of work working on the yard as well.

24

A GREAT BOOK YOU CAN'T PUT DOWN

Getting lost in a story and transported to another world is one of the greatest joys of being human. It's proof that imagination and words can create entire universes. I read many great books. Actually, I have recently read The Love Hypothesis, and it was kind of saucy at the end. I was also terrific, though, and yeah, what do you find a really great book out there you just constantly focus on that world and the people in it, drawing similarities in your life, which changes your perspective gradually as well.

25

STARGAZING ON A CLEAR NIGHT

Looking up at a sky full of stars reminds us of our small place in the vast universe, but instead of making us feel insignificant, it fills us with wonder. It's beautiful just driving away, especially during the summer full nights, and being able to look at the night sky and the stars and behold them is just such a wonderful thing; it's astonishing, really.

26

FINDING THE PERFECT PARKING SPOT

It's a tiny victory, but it makes your day just a little bit easier. Sometimes, life gives you small wins just when you need them. Imagine if you are in a rush and you need to get somewhere, whether that be the mall, a doctor's appointment, etc., and you have a perfect parking spot right there right after a person leaves. Are you able to park right from the building? It's great.

27

SEEING A RAINBOW AFTER THE RAIN

A rainbow is proof that even after the darkest storms, something beautiful can appear, just like in life. Imagine looking up at the sky after the rain, especially after a torrential downpour, and being able to see the rain, smelling the aroma of just freshly hydrated grass, being able to feel the sun on you afterward, and just being able to see your beautiful rainbow up in the sky, that's amazing.

28

THE FEELING OF ACCOMPLISHMENT AFTER FINISHING A TASK

That moment when you check something off your to-do list or finish a project is a reminder that progress, no matter how small, is always worth celebrating. It's nice to be able to complete your task, and seeing your progress throughout the day brings a sense of release.

29

WRAPPING YOURSELF IN A COZY BLANKET

A soft, warm blanket can make you feel safe like a gentle hug from the world reminding you to rest and recharge. Personally, I feel absolutely refreshed after being able to snuggle with a cozy blanket, especially when waking up and getting ready for the next day full of opportunities around the corner.

30

A HEARTFELT "I LOVE YOU"

Hearing those three words from someone who means it reminds you that love exists in all forms and that you are never truly alone. Hearing the words I love you just the most genuine thing that you could listen to from another person. Being able to express that they care so much about you rejuvenates you and energizes you to keep on going through these days, whether it be good or bad. It is such a good reminder to know that someone out there in the world loves you, whether it be parents and brother and sister or a person in this world who loves you.

31

WATCHING BABY ANIMALS PLAY

There's something pure and joyous about watching baby animals stumble, explore, and learn about the world—it's a reminder that innocence and happiness still exist. It's nice being able to see a bunch of little animals play; they can't understand who or what they are, but they are able to socialize with each other. It is beautiful to see them happy with their brothers or sisters and other animals within their group.

32

THE SCENT OF A LOVED ONE'S PERFUME OR COLOGNE

Certain scents bring back vivid memories, making you feel close to someone even if they're far away. It's proof that love lingers in the most minor ways. It's not because so many times I can remember the smell of my grandfather and my dad's cologne from a mile away. It's a nice gesture, or just nice to know that even in the depths of our minds, we can never forget the ones we love.

33

THE EXCITEMENT OF OPENING A PACKAGE

Tearing into a package, whether it's a gift or something you ordered for yourself, brings a little spark of joy—a reminder that anticipation and excitement still exist. The anticipation of receiving a package that you know would make your day and coming after a long shift or something is great. It's great to see that you know something or someone nice is waiting for you, and you're anticipating when you get home.

34

A HANDWRITTEN LETTER OR NOTE

In a digital world, a handwritten note is a rare and unique thing. It carries personality, care, and the reminder that someone took the time just for you. Personally, I always keep copies of the letters that I've received throughout the years and every letter I send you. Letter writing is even more interconnected than the use of phones and technology and stuff like that. I feel like a personal connection has been lost since we rely on these technologies, and being able to go to the old-fashioned ways of writing a letter gives us a sense of compassion and love for one another that comes out more passionately than when we send a text.

35

THE FIRST BLOOM OF SPRING FLOWERS

Seeing the first flowers of spring is proof that after every harsh winter, beauty returns. Life, like nature, is whole of cycles of renewal. Springtime, for me, is often the time of renewal, the time of being able to have a shot at life. We are able to witness some of the fresh flowers blooming from the tree or the grass green becoming greener, the tulips coming from the ground put the first flowers coming out, just another reminder that life continues and it keeps on going as a quick quote from Jurassic Park says, "life finds a way."

36

A PERFECTLY TIMED JOKE

Laughter shared at the perfect moment—when you least expect it but need it most—is a reminder that humor can brighten even the darkest days. Whether that be a recurring joker at your end or inside the work that you and your friends know, it is great to share a long laugh with them and be able to reminisce on previous times in the current times, especially if the joke lands really nicely.

37

BLOWING BUBBLES AND WATCHING THEM FLOAT

Something as simple as watching a bubble drift through the air can bring out childlike joy, reminding us to appreciate the little things. You know, the more you age, with life being so busy, and so you know quote on quote "Adult" as we grow up that I know sometimes you just need to take a step back and will he be able to appreciate the small things that you and having that child-like joy and being reminded of wonder blowing bubbles is one of the activities I can show you that they could bring that sense wonder and the sparkle in a person's eyes.

38

A RELAXING BATH WITH CANDLES

The warm water, the soft glow of candlelight—it's a moment of pure self-care, where the world slows down and you can just be. No, personally, I haven't done this, but a good friend of mine recommended that I do it once, and I guess it works out for her. Yeah, I know. I can just imagine being able to smell the aroma of your freshly lit candles and having a hot bath. Yes, and then your body relaxes, and the stress and the weight of the world come off as well, so you can feel rejuvenated afterward.

39

A DEEP, FULFILLING CONVERSATION

Talking with someone who truly understands you, where words flow effortlessly and time seems to stop, is one of the most beautiful human experiences. I've nights gone out a bunch of times. You know, people around my age would go out to parties and stuff. Sometimes, I just stay back and have profound conversations with my parents and my grandparents or other loved ones as well. And their conversations that I will never forget for as long as I can. Really, I don't wanna forget those conversations, many conversations that have shaped me into the person I grew up to be and have molded me. Personally, I always prefer having deep conversations. Personally, I prefer deep conversations with people that I love just to get to know them better.

40

THE SMELL OF BOOKS IN A LIBRARY

That rich, papery scent holds the weight of knowledge, adventure, and centuries of stories. It's a reminder that entire worlds exist within pages. It's nice to feel and smell the new book and being able to reach throughout the literature and get lost, you know, being able to get in the most extraordinary percent of the world, especially in the library. In my local library, I absolutely love it, as it gives me so many different resources to give to me within when I didn't have Internet for time or when the librarians help me search for various books and help me study and also give me a quiet place to study with a mentor teacher guide. Support your local library.

41

WITNESSING AN ACT OF KINDNESS

Seeing someone help another person, whether it's a small gesture or a grand act, reminds us that goodness exists in the world and that humanity is capable of deep compassion. I always strive to be that person who brings a sense of kindness to this world. It's great to be at all to see a random act of kindness with another person, but always aim to be that person as well, too. Doing an act of kindness to another person might not seem like something in our minds, but it means a whole lot to the person receiving your act of kindness.

42

A FAVORITE CHILDHOOD MOVIE OR TV SHOW

Rewatching something you loved as a child brings back nostalgia, comfort, and a reminder of simpler times when joy came quickly. I like watching old movies I used to co-op, watching as a kid, and being able to reminisce about those earlier days in my life. And it's nice to introduce what you love, that be your favorite movie or a TV show from the past, to your brothers and siblings who never grew up watching it, and you can show them what you love.

43

THE FEELING OF SAND BETWEEN YOUR TOES

The soft, grainy texture of sand beneath your feet connects you to nature, reminding you to slow down, breathe, and enjoy the moment. I personally can't wait for the summertime just to be able to feel the same between my toes and being able to have fun at a beach house. Our sense of touch is impressive, and we can use it to preserve our own lives.

44

A PERFECTLY COOKED MEAL

A meal that's prepared just right—whether by you or someone else—is a simple but powerful pleasure, reminding us that nourishment isn't just about food but also about care and experience. Thank God, we have a sense of taste because the greatest pleasure we have in our lives is that we are able to enjoy things to a greater extent. Being able to eat a perfectly cooked meal brings such a sense of relief, comfort, nourishment, and a sense of satisfaction, especially if you're the one who cooked it.

45

THE FIRST SNOWFALL OF WINTER

Watching fresh snowfall, untouched and peaceful, brings a sense of wonder and stillness, a reminder that the world is constantly renewing itself. Personally, for me, winter really starts when I see the first snowflakes, and being able to see the first snowflakes is a reminder of why it's cold that even during what seems to be cold hard, in better times there's a sense of beauty that we could see falling from the sky.

46

THE SATISFACTION OF POPPING BUBBLE WRAP

That tiny, oddly addictive sensation of popping each bubble is a reminder that joy can come from the most straightforward, silliest things. Even now, as an adult, I still pop the bubble wrap once I get it out of packaging. It is just a little tiny gift along with the package that I really like when I receive it.

47

WATCHING FIREFLIES ON A SUMMER NIGHT

Fireflies blinking in the dark feel like tiny bits of magic, proof that even the night has its own quiet wonders. Growing up as a kid, I remember one time when it was like a really hot summer day, but then at the nighttime, the weather dropped about 70°F, and I would see a bunch of different fire Flys coming around throughout the grass and dandelions, and I would just play with them.

48

SINGING IN THE CAR WITH FRIENDS

Belting out songs at the top of your lungs with people who don't judge you is a reminder that happiness often comes in unfiltered, unplanned moments. This is one time I went out a couple of years ago for a sports event me, and my friends were listening to my playlist in the car, and what this song was, I guess that's why they call it The Blues by Elton John. I feel like that day. We played all classic Sunday morning tunes, and we sang out to all of them. Great memories I had.

49

A COLD PILLOW ON A WARM NIGHT

That instant relief of flipping your pillow to the cool side reminds us that small comforts can make all the difference. Imagine that you can just go to bed, and you know I'm just trying to get some sleep, and then you flip over the pillow, giving instant relief.

50

SEEING SOMEONE LIGHT UP BECAUSE OF YOUR WORDS OR ACTIONS

When something you do makes someone's, face brighten with joy, gratitude, or relief, it's proof that your presence in this world matters. Like I said previously, always strive to be the person who brings joy and kindness to this world. Whether it be a stranger, loved one, friend, family member, or someone, always strive to be that person who brings acts of kindness to this world. Everybody has the power to do something in their lives, and all I can hope and pray for is that people choose to do the right thing constantly. That's our point of living: to become better each day now; we might not have the perfect body or quote on quote you're not in our physical prime, but it's always something we should strive to become a more incredible version of ourselves whether it be physically, emotionally, or intellectually speaking.

Arthur Bio

I wrote this because you should always know why there is a reason to keep on living, even during our darkest days. There are days you know it might seem impossible, on auto-pilot, or with no purpose. I encourage other people to keep finding reasons as I expand my reasons to keep living life.